HAPPY BIRTHDAY

TO

....

WITH LOVE FROM

....

And Elizabeth

HAPPY BIRTHDAY—LOVE...

Complete Series

Jane Austen

Joan Crawford

Bette Davis

Liam Gallagher

Audrey Hepburn

John Lennon

Bob Marley

Marilyn Monroe

Michelle Obama

Jackie Kennedy Onassis

Elvis Presley

Keith Richards

Frank Sinatra

Elizabeth Taylor

Oscar Wilde

HAPPY BIRTHDAY
Love, Frank

ON YOUR SPECIAL DAY

ENJOY THE WIT AND WISDOM OF

FRANK SINATRA

THE CHAIRMAN OF THE BOARD

Edited by Jade Riley

CELEBRATION BOOKS

THIS IS A CELEBRATION BOOK

Published by Celebration Books 2023
Celebration Books is an imprint of Dean Street Press

Text & Design Copyright © 2023 Celebration Books

All Rights Reserved. No part of this publication may be reproduced, stored in or transmitted in any form or by any means without the written permission of the copyright owner and the publisher of this book.

Cover by DSP

ISBN 978 1 915393 78 4

www.deanstreetpress.co.uk

HAPPY BIRTHDAY—LOVE, ELIZABETH

As the Queen of Hollywood, Elizabeth Taylor was known for her legendary birthday parties. As a child her family gathered around a simple, home-made cake, but when she married the first of her eight husbands at the age of 18, these occasions naturally stepped up to champagne, jewels and glamour. At the time of her 40th birthday, her good friend Princess Grace of Monaco was complaining how she longed to have a night away from royal duties, filled with carefree dancing. So Elizabeth (*never* Liz) and her husband, Richard Burton, rented the Hotel Intercontinental in Budapest and invited celebrities like Michael Caine, Raquel Welch and Ringo Starr to add to the fun. Her husband also marked the night by giving Elizabeth a 52-carat, sugarloaf Sapphire cabochon sautoir necklace. Just a little birthday treat to say "I love you."

1978 saw another magnificent festivity in her honor as Ms. Taylor was fêted at the legendary Studio 54 nightclub in Manhattan. Photos of her with designer Halston, singers Liza Minnelli and Elton John attest that no one was more beloved, or more famous, than Ms. Taylor. But she didn't need *le tout New York* to have a good time; she was just as happy donning cowboy boots and inviting family and friends for her

60th birthday at Disneyland. Of course, the park was closed off to all but her special guests.

Although she was famous the world over, Elizabeth was a down-to-earth soul, renowned for outstanding generosity to charity. Not surprisingly, for her 65th birthday bash she invited over 2500 people and raised $1 million dollars for AIDS research. At the event she remarked "I'm not here to celebrate my birthday. I'm here to celebrate all the people around the world with AIDS. They will be touched by your love, and I thank you so much for that." Now that's class!

Happy Birthday from the brightest star with the biggest heart, Elizabeth Taylor!

Elizabeth Taylor

Big girls need big diamonds.

"How can the money be the root of all evil when shopping is the cure for all sadness?

Pour yourself a drink, put on some lipstick, and pull yourself together.

"Follow your passions, follow your heart, and the things you need will come.

Success is a great deodorant.

"Some of my best leading men have been dogs and horses.

"People who know me well, call me Elizabeth. I dislike Liz."

I've only slept with the men I've been married to. How many women can make that claim?

I've been pronounced dead and I've read my own obituaries. And they were the best reviews I ever read.

"I used to think that drinking would help my shyness, but all it did was exaggerate all the negative qualities.

"All I see in the mirror every morning is a face that needs washing."

"I don't pretend to be an ordinary housewife.

This is how I live everywhere! Champagne and poop.

If it is not to make the world a better place, what is money for?

> Give. Remember always to give. That is the one thing that will make you grow.

You can't cry on a diamond's shoulder, and diamonds won't keep you warm at night, but they're sure fun when the sun shines.

When people say 'She's got everything', I've only one answer: I haven't had tomorrow.

Since I was a little girl, I believed I was a child of destiny, and if that is true, Richard Burton was surely my fate.

I hate the idea of always having to interpret other people's ideas and thoughts and words, because I'm very independent and, I guess, a free thinker.

"I find vocabulary to be a great drawback.

I love Johnny Depp, and I love Colin Farrell—both brilliant, nuanced actors with great range.

" You are who you are.
All you can do in this world is help others to be who they are and better themselves. "

There can be no love without respect.

"You can be fat and still be sexy. It all depends on how you feel about yourself.

Everything makes me nervous—except making films.

As a girl, my mother told me I'm nice looking and that I have pretty eyes, but it's not your eyes . . . it's the expression behind your eyes that will make you truly beautiful.

> I've always been very aware of the inner me that has nothing to do with the physical me.

"If you can't laugh at yourself, you're cooked.

"

"I believe in life and I'll fight for it. I believe you have to put up your dukes and fight, even if you don't know what you're fighting against.

" You can't dance with crazy. "

I love to be casual and comfortable, but I also love the easy glamour of wearing jewelry all the time.

" I, along with the critics, have never taken myself very seriously.

"

I wasn't allowed to date, as a result, I had no real inner self-confidence.

"The most sensible thing to do to people you hate is to drink their brandy.

"No matter what happens, I'm loud, noisy, earthy and ready for much more living.

"You find out who your real friends are when you're involved in a scandal.

"

"It's all about hope, kindness and a connection with one another.

I feel very adventurous. There are so many doors to be opened, and I'm not afraid to look behind them.

> I know I'm vulgar, but would you have me any other way?

"I don't have a short temper, I just have a quick reaction to bullshit.

It is strange that the years teach us patience; that the shorter our time, the greater our capacity for waiting.

Now is the time for guts and guile.

I've been through it all, baby, I'm mother courage.

It is dangerous to think people human, who once have been divine.

I think I'm finally growing up—and about time.

"I suppose when they reach a certain age some men are afraid to grow up. It seems the older the men get, the younger their new wives get."

"If I love someone, I love them always.

"

> How can anything bad come out of love? The bad stuff comes out of mistrust, misunderstanding and God knows from hate and from ignorance.

"I am a very committed wife. And I should be committed too—for being married so many times.

"I think marriage does give a sense of oneness that just being together can't.

So much is said with the electricity of the eyes, the intensity of a whisper.
Less is more.

"You can't possess radiance, you can only admire it.

I really don't remember much about *Cleopatra*. There were a lot of other things going on.

"When the sun comes up, I have morals again.

I don't dwell on the miserable. I skirt around that. Give it a wave. Wave goodbye and concentrate on the good things.

"Seeing one face continually in crowds is one of the minor annoyances of being in love."

When you're older, you'll appreciate the advantages of sleeping alone.

If it is love, it must encompass everything. The faults as well as the things you are proud of, and one has to be tolerant of one's intolerances.

"If someone's dumb enough to offer me a million dollars to make a picture, I'm certainly not dumb enough to turn it down."

I am glad that in my life I have never cut short my emotions. The most awful thing of all is to be numb.

It is not true that I like animals more than people. But they come a very close second. There is no bullshit about them.

"The things that are important to me—being a mother, a businesswoman, an activist—are all things that were borne out of great passion.

I've come through things that would have felled an ox. That fills me with optimism, not just for myself but for our particular species.

"Every day we need to tell someone we love them. Touch them. Thank them for being. It's so important.

"

I don't have a set pattern.
I take things as they come.
Usually with a great amount
of relish. I just lay back and
wait for it to happen. And it
usually does.

"

"
I have never felt more alive than when I watched my children delight in something, never more alive than when I have watched a great artist perform, and never richer than when I have scored a big check to fight AIDS.

"

I believe in the difference between men and women. In fact, I embrace the difference.

> Men are not forced to turn their desolation to advantage as women are. It's easier for them to dissipate their passion, quell their restlessness in other ways.

I think having a fight, an out and out outrageous, ridiculous fight is one of the greatest exercises in marital togetherness.

> I never face the day without perfume.

"You can't choose between right and wrong by taking a census.

I call upon you to draw from the depths of your being—to prove that we are a human race, to prove that our love outweighs our need to hate, that our compassion is more compelling than our need to blame.

You cannot have passion of any kind unless you have compassion.

"Every breath you take today should be with someone else in mind.

"Humility is a characteristic I expect to find in other people.

"I love life. I really love it. And I exalt in life now.

"I fell off my pink cloud with a thud."

The disaster of being old was in not feeling safe to venture anywhere, of seeing freedom put out of reach.

"One is left so much on one's own. People are shy of the bereaved. They don't quite know what to be.

"So much to do, so little done, such things to be.

"

Acting is, to me now, artificial. Seeing people suffer is real. It couldn't be more real. Some people don't like to look at it in the face because it's painful. But if nobody does, then nothing gets done.

> If you hear of me getting married [again], slap me!

"The public me, the one named Elizabeth Taylor, has become a lot of hokum and fabrication—a bunch of drivel—and I find her slightly revolting.

"I haven't read any of the autobiographies about me.

"

God damn it, you refuse to let it get to you. You fight. You cry. You curse. Then you go about the business of living. That's how I've done it. There's no other way.

"I do enjoy life,
I really do.
Especially if I wake
up the next day.

Elizabeth Taylor

ABOUT THE EDITOR

Jade Riley is a writer whose interests include old movies, art history, vintage fashion and books, books, books.

Her dream is to move to London, to write like Virginia Woolf, and to meet a man like Mr. Darcy, who owns a vacation home in Greece.

www.ingramcontent.com/pod-product-compliance
Lightning Source LLC
Chambersburg PA
CBHW030047100526
44590CB00011B/356